ANCIENT CIVILIZATIONS

ANCIENT EGYPT

L. J. AMSTUTZ

Essential Library

An Imprint of Abdo Publishing | www.abdopublishing.com

ANCIENT CIVILIZATIONS

ANCIENT
EGYPT

L. J. AMSTUTZ

CONTENT CONSULTANT

Elizabeth McGovern
Egyptologist, Adjunct Instructor
New York University

www.abdopublishing.com

Published by Abdo Publishing, a division of ABDO, PO Box 398166, Minneapolis, Minnesota 55439.
Copyright © 2015 by Abdo Consulting Group, Inc. International copyrights reserved in all countries.
No part of this book may be reproduced in any form without written permission from the publisher.
Essential Library™ is a trademark and logo of Abdo Publishing.

Printed in the United States of America, North Mankato, Minnesota

102014
012015

THIS BOOK CONTAINS
RECYCLED MATERIALS

Cover Photos: mountainpix/Shutterstock Images, foreground; Dan Breckwoldt/Shutterstock
Images, background

Interior Photos: Dan Breckwoldt/Shutterstock Images, 2; Robert Harding World Imagery/Corbis,
6–7; Everett Collection Historical/Alamy, 11, 39; Red Line Editorial, 13, 23; Gary Warnimont/Alamy,
15; iStockphoto, 16, 27, 32–33, 74–75; Bettmann/Corbis, 20; Peter Horree/Alamy, 31; Passion Images/
Shutterstock Images, 37; Elzbieta Sekowska/Shutterstock Images, 41; Photos.com/Thinkstock, 42–43,
47, 57; Prisma Archivo/Alamy, 52–53; Robert Harding Picture Library Ltd/Alamy, 59, 61; Kumar
Sriskandan/Alamy, 62–63; Thinkstock, 67; Shutterstock Images, 69, 96; Zhukov Oleg/Shutterstock
Images, 71; Dorling Kindersley/Thinkstock, 78; Glasshouse Images/Alamy, 82–83; Amanda Lewis/
iStockphoto, 87, 88; nagelstock.com/Alamy, 90–91

Editor: Rebecca Rowell
Series Designer: Jake Nordby

Library of Congress Control Number: 2014943842

Cataloging-in-Publication Data

Amstutz, L.J.
  Ancient Egypt / L.J. Amstutz.
    p. cm. -- (Ancient civilizations)
  ISBN 978-1-62403-537-1 (lib. bdg.)
  Includes bibliographical references and index.
  1. Egypt--Civilization--To 332 B.C.--Juvenile literature. 2. Egypt--History--Juvenile literature. 3. Egypt-
-Social life and customs--Juvenile literature.   I. Title.
  932--dc23

                                                            2014943842

CONTENTS

CHAPTER 1

FERTILE SOIL

The ancient Egyptians believed their pharaohs were reincarnations of Horus, the god of light, in human form. That made Tutankhaten—or King Tut, as people know him today—divine. As a pharaoh, Tut was responsible for maintaining *ma'at*, or order and harmony, in Egypt. This was a daunting task for someone who was only nine years old.

King Tut's funerary mask has become a symbol of Egypt past and present.

King Tut's Mask

Howard Carter found King Tut in the innermost chamber of Tut's tomb. The ancient pharaoh's mummy lay inside three nested coffins. The innermost one was made of solid gold. A magnificent solid gold mask covered the young pharaoh's face, bearing the royal insignia of Upper Egypt and Lower Egypt—a vulture and a serpent, respectively. The mask's expression is serene. The beauty and appeal of the young pharaoh's face have made it the best-known artifact found in the tomb and a symbol of the splendor of ancient Egypt. Today, King Tut's mask shines as brightly as ever at the Egyptian Museum in Cairo, Egypt.

Tut took the throne in 1333 BCE. As a member of the royal family, Tut would have been well prepared for his role as pharaoh. Young royals studied reading, writing, literature, mathematics, and foreign languages. Their schooling included athletics such as archery, ball games, boating, swimming, and wrestling. In his spare time, Tut may have played in the courtyards with his many half brothers and half sisters, swam, and fished in the Nile. Tut likely enjoyed a game of *senet.* As royalty, he ate and drank the finest foods and wines the land provided and lived in a palace filled with beautiful statues and wall paintings.

Perhaps as an attempt to bring order and harmony to Egypt, or simply as a political move, Tut set about restoring the gods his predecessor, Akhenaten, had banished, especially Amun, king of the gods. Akhenaten had forced his people to worship only one god: Aten, the sun disk. Young Tut not only brought back the old gods and temples his father had banned, he changed his name from Tutankhaten to Tutankhamen, or "living image of Amun."[1]

These acts were the most significant of the young pharaoh's rule. He died while still a teenager in 1323 BCE. He lay nearly forgotten for thousands of years, until Howard Carter discovered Tut's tomb in 1922 CE. Although robbers had entered in ancient times, fabulous riches remained in Tut's tomb. While he was relatively unimportant as a ruler during his life, the treasures in his tomb made King Tut the best-known Egyptian of all time and

Egyptomania

Egyptomania—fascination with ancient Egypt—dates as far back as the 300s BCE to ancient Greece. The ancient Romans were interested in Egypt, too. Roman emperors in the first centuries CE collected Egyptian statues and obelisks and built their own Egyptian-style statues and buildings. The Romans even built pyramid tombs and worshiped some of the Egyptian gods.

Few Europeans visited Egypt from 641 CE, when it came under Islamic rule, until the late 1600s, but people continued to study and imitate the Egyptian artifacts already in Europe. When the French military commander Napoléon Bonaparte invaded Egypt in 1798, taking along scholars as well as soldiers, Egyptomania exploded again and continued throughout the 1800s. Howard Carter's discovery of King Tut's tomb in 1922 fanned the flames. Today, the mummies, pyramids, and other artifacts of this ancient culture continue to intrigue people.

The Nile valley, the valley in which the Nile River flows, is 660 miles (1,062 km) long. Its floodplain covers 4,250 square miles (11,000 sq km). Its width varies from 1.25 miles (2 km) to 11 miles (18 km). At the mouth of the river, where the Nile joins the Mediterranean Sea, is a wide triangle of wet, fertile land called a delta. The Nile delta covers approximately 8,500 square miles (22,000 sq km).[3]

reignited the world's fascination with the mysterious culture of ancient Egypt.

THE GIFT OF THE NILE

"Egypt is the gift of the Nile," wrote one of the world's first historians, the Greek Herodotus.[2] The Nile River was the lifeblood of ancient Egypt—so vital, the people thought it divine. Each year, after heavy tropical rains fell in Ethiopia to the south, the Nile burst its banks during the inundation, or flooding. When the floodwaters receded, they left behind fertile black soil for growing crops. The Nile also provided an abundance of fish and waterfowl, a means of transportation, and papyrus reeds for making papyrus, a precursor to paper.

Stretching 4,132 miles (6,650 km) from beginning to end, the Nile is the world's longest river. It is one of the few rivers that flow north instead of south. Since the water flows downstream to the sea, the Egyptians called the southern part of their country Upper Egypt and the northern part Lower Egypt.

The Egyptians called their country Kemet, "black land."[4] They named it for the black, life-giving soil in the floodplain. They called the desert around them Deshret, "red land."[5] The ancient Egyptians saw the desert as chaotic, with its wild animals and the desert tribes who spoke other languages. They saw the barren landscape as sacred, too, by burying their dead in cemeteries there. The desert also brought life, as the source of many needed materials and wild game. Egyptians hunted elephants, gazelles, lions, and rabbits there. The desert provided other resources. The eastern desert held copper ore, and the desert hills near the Nile valley provided the granite, limestone, and sandstone used for building temples and tombs. The deserts also

ANCIENT EGYPT (1400s BCE)

contained rarer materials, such as alabaster, diorite, emeralds, gold, marble, and turquoise.

LASTING IDEAS

The Egyptian civilization made great advances in farming, timekeeping, mathematics, architecture, and medicine that spread throughout the ancient world and led to further discoveries. Its burial methods and desert climate provided nearly perfect conditions to preserve its history for thousands of years. Few, if any, civilizations have been so well preserved.

Ancient Egypt laid the foundation for much modern knowledge about medicine and mathematics, developed the precursor to paper, and gave the world items people use today, such as glass. And many of these innovations were thanks to the Nile valley, which provided fertile soil for crops and inspired ideas.

A recreation of King Tut's burial chamber brings some of Egypt's ancient history to life.

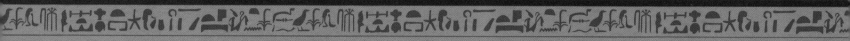

A CLOSER LOOK

KING TUT'S TOMB

For more than 30 years, Howard Carter had been digging in the sweltering Egyptian desert. He had found some important artifacts and tombs. He wanted to find one missing tomb: that of Tutankhamen, the boy king. Carter convinced the Earl of Carnarvon, who had a keen interest in Egyptology, to pay for the expedition. The team dug for five years and found very little. Carter convinced Carnarvon to try one last time in 1922 CE.

After five days, while excavating near the tomb of Ramses IV, a sudden silence alerted Carter that something had happened. Workers had found a step. More digging revealed a sunken stairway and a still-sealed doorway. Carter quickly sent a message to Carnarvon: "At last have made wonderful discovery in Valley; a magnificent tomb with seals intact; re-covered same for your arrival; congratulations."[6]

Once Carnarvon arrived, workers dug through the cluttered passageway and found a second doorway. Robbers had entered the tomb in ancient times, but the doors had been resealed. After making a hole large enough to enter, Carter peered inside. As his eyes adjusted to the light, he began to see objects and "everywhere the glint of gold."[7]

Carter and his team found more than 600 groups of objects in the tomb's four rooms, including chariots, couches, vases, stools, chests, and a throne—everything the pharaoh could possibly need in the next life. Workers needed more than ten years to remove all the treasures.

CHAPTER 2

THRIVING IN A DESERT

For all its accomplishments in knowledge and materials, ancient Egypt is remarkable for something more: its long existence. The civilization lasted for almost 3,000 years, from 3100 to 30 BCE. Few civilizations have existed as long with so little change.

Today, the Nile River continues to bring life to the desert.

Ancient Egypt's geography kept it isolated from far-away cultures. Surrounded by deserts to the east and west, the Mediterranean Sea to the north, and large boulders blocking the Nile to the south, Egypt was almost a world unto itself. The ancient Egyptians traded with their close neighbors to the north and south. They also fought with them regularly, especially with the Nubians to the south, but the Egyptians were not explorers.

Another effect of Egypt's geography was that its boundaries changed very little over time. However, as the Egyptians developed better irrigation techniques, they extended their usable land farther into the desert. And as they conquered foreign lands, the Egyptians' influence grew to include a wider area.

Ancient Egyptian history can be divided into four major eras—kingdoms separated by intermediate periods of chaos. It can also be divided into 30 dynasties, or lines of pharaohs. The first dynasty began more than 5,000 years ago.

THE PREDYNASTIC PERIOD

Pottery fragments, stone tools, and other artifacts show people settled the Nile valley in approximately 5000 BCE, when the surrounding grasslands turned to desert. Before that time, the climate was wetter. Archaeologists have found the remains of trees and animals buried in the desert sands.

Huge Nile floods made the valley unlivable. Groups of people who were hunters and gatherers roamed the Sahara Desert to the west of the Nile and lived near the shores of the Red Sea to the east. As the climate became drier, they moved into the Nile valley. There, they found plentiful fish, birds, crocodiles, hippos, ibex, and wild cattle to hunt. They learned to harness the Nile waters to grow crops in the fertile soil.

During the predynastic period (c. 5000–2926 BCE), the Egyptians established small kingdoms along the Nile valley that eventually became known as the northern Red Land and the southern White Land. Each area had its own king and gods. Scholars know little about this period because no one has discovered written records.

THE EARLY DYNASTIC PERIOD

Ancient Egyptian history begins with the early dynastic period (c. 2925–2575 BCE). This period started when a strong leader called Narmer united the kingdoms by conquering the north. Memphis

The Narmer Palette

One of Egypt's most important artifacts is the Narmer Palette, a stone tablet from approximately 3100 BCE that tells the story of Narmer, the first ruler of unified Egypt. The intricately carved tablet shows the king's godlike status, depicting him both as a wild bull trampling the enemy and a victorious king, still wearing a bull's tail. On the front, he holds a mace, ready to strike an enemy. On the back, rows of dead enemies lie with their heads between their legs.

became the first capital of unified Egypt.

The name Narmer means "raging catfish."[1] Egyptians considered the catfish brave and aggressive, so this was high praise. Narmer ruled for 62 years, until he was killed by a hippo during a hunting trip. The early dynastic period was followed by the Old Kingdom period, which was the great age of the pyramids.

The Narmer Palette, a stone tablet from the time of Narmer, remains in almost perfect condition.

THE OLD KINGDOM

The Old Kingdom lasted from approximately 2575 to 2130 BCE and was an era of peace and splendor. Its grand building projects and the unmatched power of the pharaohs set it apart from other periods of Egypt's ancient history. The people worshiped the sun god Re, also spelled Ra, along with many other gods and goddesses. The ancient Egyptians considered the pharaohs god-kings. The pharaohs held absolute power over their subjects. Only the pharaohs could be certain of eternal life. To aid their journey to the underworld after death, pharaohs of the first two dynasties built mastabas, which were large rectangular tombs.

Djoser was the first to build a new style of tomb, designed by an architect named Imhotep. Known as the Step Pyramid, it was initially built in approximately 2630 as a mastaba. By 2611, it rose 200 feet (61 m) into the air and looked like six mastabas stacked on top of each other. This launched the age of pyramids, and later pharaohs built larger and larger monuments.

Pyramid design improved with each generation. Sneferu was the first pharaoh to use smooth sides. First, he built a step pyramid larger than any previous pyramid. Not content with that monument, he built a second pyramid—the first one with smooth sides. The design's steep angles made the pyramid unstable, and it nearly collapsed. During construction, workers adjusted the structure. Today, it is known as the Bent Pyramid. Sneferu achieved what he wanted on his third try: the Red Pyramid, so named for the red granite on its surface. He was likely buried in this pyramid.

In approximately 2550 BCE, Sneferu's son, Khufu, built the most famous pyramid: the Great Pyramid at Giza, just outside modern Cairo. At 481 feet (147 m), it remained the tallest structure in the world for 4,500 years, until the Eiffel Tower was built in 1889 CE. Its 755-foot- (230 m) wide base is longer than two football fields. The Great Pyramid is the only one of the Seven Wonders of the Ancient World still standing. It took 2.3 million stones and 20 years to build.[2] Khufu also built a temple to himself. Five large pits near the structures held boats to carry his body and possessions to the underworld.

Khufu's son, Khafre, built a pyramid ten feet (3 m) shorter than his father's, but it looked taller because it was built on higher ground. In approximately 2500 BCE, Khafre also built the Great Sphinx, a creature with the body of a lion and the head of a man.

All these building projects required massive amounts of labor and resources, which eventually took a toll on the country. Later pharaohs could not match these monuments' sizes without risking a revolt by the people. Still, pharaohs continued building impressive monuments, including smaller

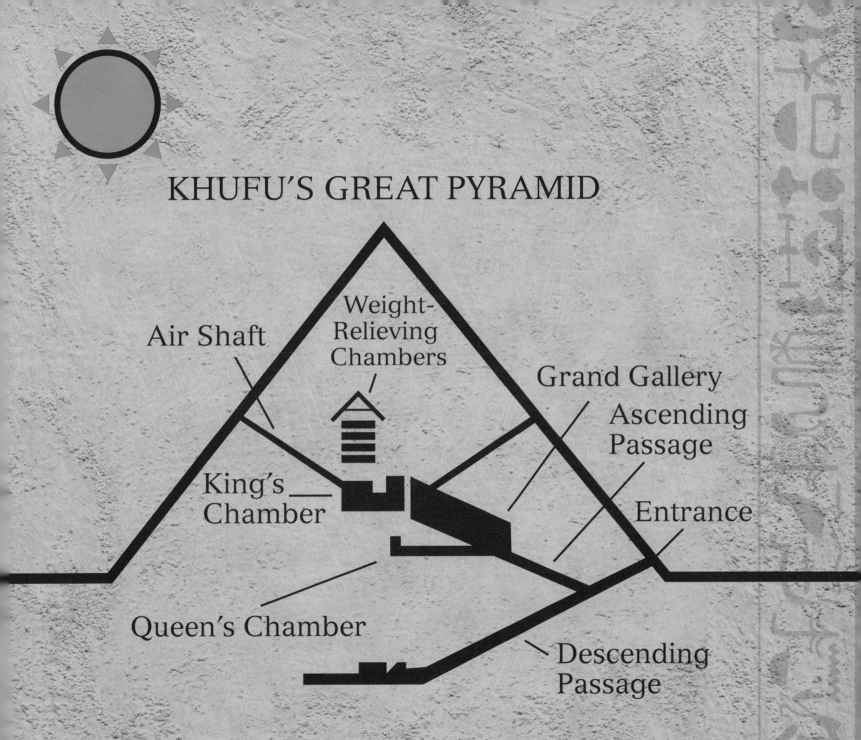

KHUFU'S GREAT PYRAMID

Air Shaft

Weight-Relieving Chambers

Grand Gallery

Ascending Passage

King's Chamber

Entrance

Queen's Chamber

Descending Passage

23

pyramids, temples dedicated to the sun, and obelisks, which are towering shafts of rock with a pyramid-shaped top.

Egypt's longest-ruling pharaoh, Pepi II, ruled near the end of the Old Kingdom, from age six to 100 (2269–2175 BCE). His daughter, Nitocris, took over after his death. When she died, things fell apart. Egypt split into several smaller warring states. Its irrigation systems deteriorated, and thieves broke into the pyramids. Several years of little rain caused famine and starvation, and the desert threatened to reclaim the fertile land. During this period, Egyptians questioned their basic beliefs in the gods and pharaohs.

The Seven Wonders of the Ancient World

Similar to today's travel guides, ancient Greek and Roman writings listed great manmade wonders every traveler should see. The lists varied, but the seven sites most often noted are known today as the Seven Wonders of the Ancient World:

• Pyramids at Giza, Egypt

• Hanging Gardens of Babylon, modern-day Iraq exact location unknown

• Temple of Artemis at Ephesus, modern-day Turkey

• Giant statue of Zeus at Olympia, Greece

• Mausoleum at Halicarnassus, modern-day Turkey

• Colossus of Rhodes, a massive statue in the Aegean Sea honoring Helios, the sun god

• Lighthouse of Alexandria on the island of Pharos, near Egypt

This period of chaos is known as the first intermediate period. It lasted from approximately 2130 to 1938 BCE. One papyrus, its author unknown, describes the time:

The bowman is ready. The wrongdoer is everywhere. . . . A man goes out to plow with his shield. . . . A man looks upon his son as his enemy. A man smites his brother, his mother's son. Men sit in the bushes until the benighted traveler comes, in order to plunder his load. . . . Men's hearts are violent. The plague is throughout the land. Blood is everywhere.[3]

The golden age of the Old Kingdom rulers had come to an end. Egypt would never be quite the same.

THE MIDDLE KINGDOM

After such a painful period, Egypt was in desperate need of another strong leader. In 1938 BCE, Amenemhet I unified Egypt again and began another era of strength and prosperity. The Middle Kingdom would last until approximately 1630 BCE.

During this era, the military grew stronger and the arts flourished. The Egyptians built a massive irrigation works to make the most efficient use of the Nile floods. The pharaohs continued building pyramids during the Middle Kingdom. The monuments were smaller than those of the Old Kingdom and contained twisting passageways, hidden chambers, and traps to thwart tomb

The Great Sphinx

The Great Sphinx is a giant sculpture with the body of a lion and the head of a man—probably Khafre. The Egyptians carved it in approximately 2520 BCE. Excavations in 1978 CE uncovered some of the tools used to carve the head and neck.

Today, the Sphinx looks quite different from when it was built. Arabs broke off its nose in the 400s CE because they considered the sculpture a pagan image. It originally had a beard, pieces of which archaeologists found in 1817. Evidence also shows the Sphinx had stripes of bright yellow and blue paint on its headdress. In 1998, a conservation program finished restoring the Great Sphinx.

robbers. Nonroyals began building huge tombs of their own during this era. And the Egyptians built large fortresses along the Nile to the south of Egypt.

Succeeding pharaohs were not strong enough leaders to hold the kingdom together, however. They lost control of the southern fortresses, and competing kings took over parts of the delta. The second intermediate period (1630–1540 BCE) followed the Middle Kingdom when the Hyksos, "rulers of foreign lands," took over all Egypt except for a small area near Thebes, which is a city in Upper Egypt.[4] During this era, Egypt had 160 kings, and the capital moved several times.

The Hyksos probably introduced horses, chariots, and stronger bows to Egypt. These conquerors adopted the Egyptian way of life, including building temples to the gods and wearing Egyptian clothing. Still, the Egyptians considered them "vile Asiatics," according to an inscription by Kamose, one of three princes of Thebes, who waged war on the Hyksos.[5] His successor, Ahmose, drove

The pharaoh wore crowns symbolizing control of Egypt: white for Upper Egypt, red for Lower Egypt, and the two together for the unified lands.

out the Hyksos in 1539 and restored Egypt to native rule, launching a new era in ancient Egypt's history.

THE NEW KINGDOM

When Ahmose reunited Egypt, the age of empire, known as the New Kingdom (1539–1075 BCE), began. The Egyptians used what they had learned from the Hyksos to make better chariots and weapons. The Egyptians realized they needed to control their neighbors to prevent another invasion. They began taking over neighboring lands, including Phoenicia, Palestine,

Syria, and Nubia. They demanded an annual payment of goods called tribute from each conquered land.

The New Kingdom rulers repaired the old temples and built new ones. They did not build pyramids, perhaps to avoid tomb robbers. Instead, they carved tombs in the cliffs of the Valley of the Kings near Thebes. They sealed the tombs and swore all the workers to secrecy. However, robbers eventually found nearly all these tombs. Most were robbed in ancient times—the wealth inside was simply too great a temptation to workers, thieves, and even government officials. Somewhere between 1075 BCE and 945 BCE, priests moved many of the royal mummies to secret tombs to protect them. They remained hidden until the late 1800s CE.

One notable New Kingdom pharaoh was Amenhotep IV, or Akhenaten, who ruled from 1353 to 1336 BCE. He forced everyone to worship only one god: the Aten. Citizens were not pleased with his decision. Tutankhamen, Akhenaten's son, ruled from 1333 to 1323 BCE and restored the old gods before he died, and life went on much as it had before.

Tutankhamen's death ended the royal bloodline—he had no children to succeed him. Two of his officials ruled next, then Ramses I became pharaoh in 1292 BCE, beginning a new dynasty. He had first served as a soldier, vizier, and high priest of Amun under Horemheb, the second pharaoh to serve after

Tutankhamen. Ramses I became pharaoh when Horemheb died without an heir. Ramses I ruled only two years, until 1290 BCE.

Ramses II, Ramses I's grandson, made a name for himself by completing the giant hall at Karnak, building mammoth statues of himself and carving his own name on earlier monuments. He had many wives and more than 100 children. Ramses II may be the pharaoh mentioned in the book of Exodus in the Old Testament. He ruled from 1279 to 1213 BCE.

Another interesting New Kingdom pharaoh was Hatshepsut, who ruled from 1473 to 1458 BCE. This female pharaoh took the throne when

Egyptology

Egyptology is the study of all things pertaining to ancient Egypt, including its architecture, art, history, language, literature, and religion. Some have called Prince Khaemwaset, the son of Ramses II (1279–1213 BCE), the first Egyptologist because he restored some of the old pyramids and excavated burial sites of some sacred bulls. Early historians, such as Herodotus, who lived in the 400s BCE, traveled through Egypt and recorded what they learned.

Egyptology grew most rapidly in the late 1800s CE, as new archaeological techniques developed and fabulous finds riveted the world. Beginning in 1880, Sir William Matthew Flinders Petrie likely made more discoveries than any other archaeologist, and his careful scientific methods greatly influenced the field of Egyptology. Today, many universities offer programs in Egyptology.

Tuthmose III, her stepson, was named pharaoh at a young age. She ruled well and often portrayed herself as a king in statues, even wearing the traditional false beard of the pharaohs. After her death, Tuthmose III erased her name and knocked down her statues. He went on to become one of Egypt's greatest rulers, known for his great military power and major building programs.

As the Egyptian empire became more powerful and wealthy, a new problem developed. Much of the wealth went to the god Amun, so his priests became very rich and powerful. At the end of the New Kingdom, the high priests of Amun seized control of the south, and Egypt split again. Ramses XI was the last pharaoh of this period. His death in 1075 BCE brought the New Kingdom to a close.

The following period of chaos, which lasted from 1075 to 656 BCE, is known as the third intermediate period. During this period, the Libyans invaded. The Assyrians invaded as well and installed their own rulers over all Egypt.

THE LATE PERIOD

Egypt would never regain its former glory and independence. Following the Assyrians, the Persians took over Egypt during the late period (664–332 BCE). They put a satrap, or governor, in charge of Egypt. Toward the end of this period, native rulers managed to regain control for a short time, but the Persians defeated them again.

In 332 BCE, Alexander the Great of Greece invaded Egypt. The Egyptians welcomed him because they hated the Persians. When Alexander died a few years later, one of his generals, Ptolemy, took the throne. He and his descendants claimed the title and role of pharaoh, ruling just as the Egyptian pharaohs of the past had. During this time, these Greek rulers built the Library of Alexandria and Egypt became an important center of learning. Queen Cleopatra VII was the last of this line to rule before Augustus conquered Egypt in 30 BCE and made it part of the Roman Empire. Ancient Egyptian culture ended more than 400 years later, in 391 CE, when the arrival of Christianity outlawed polytheism in Egypt.

A carving in the temple at Dandarah, Egypt, depicts Cleopatra, Egypt's last pharaoh.

CHAPTER 3

KINGS, CLASSES, AND COMMERCE

An Egyptian pharaoh had an incredible amount of power. The pharaoh, who was usually but not always male, was the ultimate ruler of Egypt. He was considered a god—the falcon-headed Horus, king of the living, in human form. When the pharaoh

The Temple of Hatshepsut in Luxor, Egypt, honors one of Egypt's few female pharaohs.

approached lower-class people, they lay face down at his feet. Even the upper classes knelt down and touched their heads to the ground. No one could speak to the pharaoh unless he gave them permission. The earliest pharaohs owned all the land. Gradually, they gave some of it to temples and families who had worked the land for generations, so over time, the pharaoh owned less property.

Female Pharaohs

Although men generally ruled ancient Egypt, at least five women served as pharaoh. One of the most successful was Hatshepsut, who took power when her husband, Tuthmose II, died in 1473 BCE. First, she ruled on behalf of her young stepson, who was to inherit the throne. After six years, she proclaimed herself pharaoh and wore a false beard and male clothing on occasions. She seemed to be popular with the priests and officials. The people called her "beautiful to behold."[1] Hatshepsut built a huge temple and other monuments to herself. She ruled until her death in 1458 BCE.

After Hatshepsut's death, her stepson Tuthmose III became pharaoh. Later in his career, he tried to erase Hatshepsut from history by chiseling her name off the monuments and smashing her statues, possibly to ensure his own son's claim to the throne. He did not completely succeed in erasing her. In 1903 CE, Howard Carter found Hatshepsut's sarcophagus in one of the tombs in the Valley of the Kings. However, her mummy was not inside. In 2005, Egyptologist Zahi Hawass and a team of scientists tentatively identified a naked mummy found elsewhere as Hatshepsut, based on a missing tooth that matched one found in a container labeled as Hatshepsut's liver.

Male pharaohs usually had many wives, and so did some Egyptian citizens. The pharaoh chose one of the wives to be the "great royal wife."[2] Her sons were next in line to the throne. Royal children often married their own siblings to maintain the royal bloodlines and increase their chances of becoming pharaoh.

While people today use the word *pharaoh* for the Egyptian kings, the Egyptians called their ruler *nesu-bit*. The word *pharaoh* comes from the Egyptian word *per ah*, which means "great house."[3] It referred to the royal palace.

The crook and flail symbolized a pharaoh's power and were often pictured on tombs and other monuments. For example, King Tut's coffin shows a crook and flail crossed on his chest. The crook showed he was the shepherd of his people; the flail represented his power. The pharaoh's responsibilities included preserving *ma'at*, the order and harmony of the universe. He kept away chaos by fighting off enemies. He made offerings to the gods to protect the country and cause the Nile to flood. The pharaoh was the high priest in every temple and visited the important state temples and cult centers regularly. He had absolute authority over the country and made decisions about laws, trade, and relationships with other countries.

Egyptians treated the pharaoh like a god even after his death, believing he became the god Osiris. They carefully mummified and buried his body with everything he might need for his journey to the afterlife. There, he would sail the heavens with the gods.

THE UPPER CLASS

Ancient Egypt's upper class was wealthy and well educated. This group included scribes, government officials, noblemen, priests, and priestesses. Originally, all government workers were relatives of the pharaoh, but this changed as the population grew and positions started to be passed from father to son. By the time the Old Kingdom ended, the pharaoh

Servants for the Dead

The ancient Egyptians believed people journeyed to the underworld after death, where everyone had to do menial labor. They buried wealthy people with small figurines called *ushabti* that were supposed to magically come alive and work for them when needed. Archaeologists found 700 ushabti in the tomb of Pharaoh Seti I (1306–1290 BCE) when they opened it in 1817 CE.

The word *ushabti* probably comes from an Egyptian word meaning "to reply" or "answer."[4] These model farmers carried hoes and baskets. Each overseer carried a whip. Originally, the ancient Egyptians made ushabti of wood. Later, they crafted the figurines of metal, clay, or stone. Other kinds of tomb models showed servants farming or fishing and included homes, herds, granaries, and slaughterhouses.

chose nonroyals for most of these positions.

Second only to the pharaoh were one or two viziers. They oversaw the pharaoh's affairs. The viziers were responsible for the justice system and directed the pharaoh's building projects. They also oversaw the legal system, regional governors, tax collection, and the treasury.

Priests and priestesses took care of the gods and made offerings and prayers to them to help keep chaos at bay. Three times a day, they recited prayers, carefully dressed the statue of each god, applied makeup and perfumes to it, and offered it a meal. They also officiated at

Hatshepsut holds the crook and flail in this statue at her temple in Luxor, Egypt.

funerals. Most priests served only one month each year, then returned to their regular jobs, including working as civil servants or craftsmen.

Scribes were highly educated and powerful. Learning the hundreds of hieroglyphs that made up the civilization's language took up to ten years. These men also studied astronomy, astrology, mathematics, practical arts, games, and sports. Discipline was harsh—a proverb of the time noted that "a boy's ear is on his back; he only listens to the man who beats him."[5]

Ranking below the government officials and priests but above the peasants were the craftsmen and artisans. They crafted furniture, jewelry, clothing, pottery, and other daily necessities for both the living and the dead.

THE LOWER CLASSES

The lower classes consisted of farmers, unskilled laborers, serfs who served the owner of the land they farmed, and slaves. These last two groups probably made up 80 percent of the population.[6]

In Egypt's early years, slavery did not exist. But as Egypt started conquering the lands around it, prisoners of war became slaves. Children born to slaves or serfs inherited their parents' social status. Ordinary citizens could also become slaves if they could not pay their debts. Slaves could be bought and sold; however, they were able to own property and even

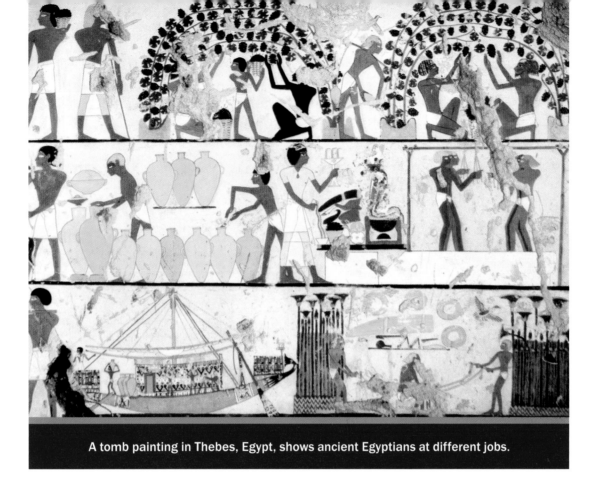

A tomb painting in Thebes, Egypt, shows ancient Egyptians at different jobs.

hire servants. Slave men could marry free women. Children born to a slave mother also became slaves.

The lower classes provided the food, resources, and labor to support the entire country of Egypt. For farmers, life revolved around the planting and harvest seasons. They worked in their fields all year except during the inundation, when they often worked for the pharaoh, building royal burial sites, mining in the desert, or serving in the military.

LOCAL GOVERNMENT

Ancient Egypt was divided into 42 *nomes*, or provinces. A *nomarch*—almost like a local king—governed each nome. He oversaw *kenbets*, which were local councils that served as a court system for all but the most serious crimes.

The law generally treated people equally, and punishments were quite severe. Consequences for minor crimes included property seizure and beatings. A dishonest official might lose a hand. Someone who shared a military secret might have his or her tongue cut out. Serious criminals were sentenced to hard labor in the mines or exiled. Those sentenced to the death penalty might be fed to crocodiles or burned alive. In later times, if someone disputed the kenbet's verdict, the council would call on the statue of a god to make the final judgment. Council members would perform ceremonies in front of the god and watch for a sign.

TAXATION AND TRADE

The treasury collected taxes from everyone. Rather than calculate how much people produced each year, the viziers measured the height of the Nile flood using a nilometer—steps built into the riverbank to show the height of the water. This told them how much each nome should have been able to produce. They taxed each farmer based on this amount.

Egypt did not have a monetary system. Citizens could pay their taxes in animals, crops, or other products. The government traded some of the items received or used them to pay state officials. Grains were stored in case of famine.

Even without a currency, Egyptian officials kept quite good records of what they produced and the taxes they collected. They traded with people from other lands, exporting cereals, dried fish, paper, and textiles and importing copper, silver, spices, and wood.

The steps of this nilometer in Upper Egypt once helped officials determine taxes.

CHAPTER 4

A DAY IN THE LIFE

The ancient Egyptians enjoyed life. In some ways, they were quite similar to people today. They worked, played, ate, drank, fell in love, and cared for their pets. But in other ways, their life was quite different.

Queen Nefertari, who lived in the 1200s BCE, plays senet, a popular board game in ancient Egypt.

43

Celebrations

Most Egyptians, especially the lower classes, worked extremely hard every day. The Egyptians did not have weekends, but they did celebrate special holy days to honor various gods. On these days, everyone went to that god's temple for a parade of idols through the streets or down the Nile, followed by a feast. During one major festival, the Feast of Opet, they celebrated for 24 days in honor of Amun and other gods.

At the end of the Egyptian year, during the Five Yearly Days, the Egyptians celebrated the ending of one year and beginning of the next, much like New Year's Eve and New Year's Day today. Festivals also celebrated natural events, such as the rise and fall of the Nile or the new moon.

GENDER ROLES

Marriage and family were very important to the ancient Egyptians. Men usually married in their twenties, and women married between ages 12 and 14. Life-spans at that time were shorter than today. Peasants often died by age 35, due to disease, accidents, hard labor, or poor nutrition. Life was a little easier for wealthier people, who might have lived 50 to 60 years.

The ancient Egyptians treated women more equally compared to other cultures of the time. Women could own property—even after they married—and were considered equal under the law. In cases of divorce, the husband had to provide for his wife, and she kept her own property. Still, job options were lacking. For the most part, women were limited to sewing, cooking, and managing the household. However, some joined the priesthood. Some women served as priestesses in the temples, servants, musicians, or dancers. A few women rose to great power, and five even became pharaoh.

Female pharaohs were considered female kings, not queens, because the title king was given to anyone ruling and was not gender specific. They were often shown wearing kingly garments and headgear, and they even wore false beards like the male pharaohs wore.

Most boys did not go to school. Children learned religion, morals, and practical life skills from their parents. Boys received training in a trade as needed. At age 14, they would begin working as apprentices or with their fathers. Only upper-class boys and those from royal families went to school. These boys became scribes, government officials, or priests.

Fun and Games

Senet was a popular board game in ancient Egypt. The game board had a grid and hieroglyphic markings. No one today is 100 percent certain about the rules, though scholars are fairly sure. Players probably tried to reach the square marked with the symbol for happiness and beauty. Each player started with five or seven playing pieces and tossed knucklebones or casting sticks before each move, just as players toss dice in some games today. Four senet boards were buried with young King Tut.

Along with board games, Egyptian children played with dolls, toy animals, balls, and slingshots. Boys fished, played games, ran races, and wrestled. Adults, especially the wealthy, enjoyed harpooning fish, hunting wild game in the desert, shooting at targets, throwing javelins, and wrestling. Adults also enjoyed board games, including senet. Although peasants had little time for play, they seem to have enjoyed talking and singing throughout the workday.

Egyptian Bread

Bread was the ancient Egyptians' most important food. Farmers grew and processed wheat, which women ground into flour with a rolling pin on a stone or, in later times, on a hollowed-out table. The women then mixed in some water, kneaded the dough, and added a pinch of day-old dough containing yeast. Next, they shaped it into loaves and baked it. The resulting bread was tasty and nutritious, but it often caused serious tooth problems. Bits of sand and grit from the grinding process wore down people's teeth, which could become infected. Egyptian doctors did not do much dentistry but may have drilled holes in the jaw to drain these abscesses. People also chewed balls of natron—the salt used in making mummies.

Upper-class girls had a different form of education. They learned about sewing. They also studied some reading and writing in an environment more relaxed than the boys.

FARMING AND FOOD

Egyptian farming methods were quite advanced for their time. Providing food for a growing population kept many Egyptians busy. Because so little land was suitable for growing crops, they took great care with it. A complex irrigation system carried water as far out from the Nile as possible. Earthen dikes divided the land into plots for each farmer, and a system of canals carried water to each plot. There, farmers used devices called shadoofs to lift the water out of the canal to the field. These posts held a cross pole with a container on one end and a counterweight on the other so the farmer could easily lift the water and swing it around to pour on his land. The government maintained the irrigation system and kept a supply of stored food for times of need.

An ancient figurine shows an Egyptian baker kneading dough.

The early Egyptians discovered that vegetables and wild grains grew from seeds and learned to plant seeds where they wanted crops to grow. Their staple crops were wheat and barley, from which they made bread and beer. Farmers planted grains in autumn, after the annual inundation of the Nile. They scattered seed over the soil, plowed it in lightly, and then used livestock to trample it into the ground. In spring, they harvested the grain with wooden sickles and tied it into bundles to carry to the threshing area. Animals trampled the grain to crack open the heads; then workers tossed the trampled grains high in the air so the chaff, or husks, would blow away. The straw was used for making brick.

Rich Egyptians ate a fairly healthy diet. Along with their staples of bread and beer, they ate a good variety of produce. Fruits included dates, figs, grapes, and pomegranates. Vegetables included cucumbers, lettuces, onions, and radishes. The Egyptians also ate beans, chickpeas, and lentils. They grew many spices, such as anise, celery seed, cumin, dill, mint, mustard, and sage, and they kept bees for honey.

Protein came from numerous sources. Farmers raised cows, oxen, sheep, gazelles, goats, oryx (a type of antelope), geese, ducks, cranes, and pigeons for meat. Cattle and goats also provided milk. Egyptians of all classes hunted birds and fished. Once chariots came into use, some hunted larger game, including elephants, leopards, lions, ostriches, and wild cattle in the desert.

Peasants could not afford to eat much meat and probably ate it only for celebrations, if at all—mainly poultry and fish. The rest of the time, they ate beans. Wealthier Egyptians enjoyed much more variety in their diet. Priests enjoyed beef.

CLOTHING AND ACCESSORIES

Most ancient Egyptians wore clothing made of linen. They made linen from the flax plant, which grew well in the marshy areas near the Nile. The fine, lightweight cloth felt pleasant in the hot climate. Most was white. Egyptians sometimes colored cloth yellow, red, and blue using natural plant and mineral dyes, but this was an expensive luxury. Cotton was not an option until Roman times. The Egyptians wore wool occasionally.

Wealthy men and kings often wore a linen kilt, or skirt, that reached to the knee. Peasants simply wore loincloths. Babies generally wore nothing at all, and children did not wear clothes until puberty. Most people wore sandals made of rush or papyrus.

The Egyptians loved jewelry. Both sexes wore it to adorn themselves, to show their wealth and status, to honor service or bravery, and, most important, to protect themselves with magic against danger, disease, and death. Amulets were popular. These charms often took the form of sacred symbols, such as the scarab beetle or the ankh, a cross with a loop at the top that symbolized life. The Eye of Horus—a symbol of wisdom, health, and prosperity—was thought to hold especially potent magic.

Men and women also used a lot of makeup and perfume. They created special creams to remove spots and wrinkles and used razors, tweezers,

Perfumes

Ancient Egypt was a hot, sweaty place, but that did not mean people smelled bad. The Egyptians were expert perfume makers and even exported perfumes. One famous variety called Oil of Lilies contained 1,000 lilies in each batch. When attending parties, people often placed wax cones scented with perfumes and spices on their heads. These cones released a pleasant scent as they slowly melted in the Egyptian heat.

or creams to remove body hair. They also used ground carob beans as a deodorant.

Ancient Egyptian paintings show that both men and women wore large amounts of eye paint. The paint was originally made of malachite, or green copper ore, and later of galena, or lead ore. Not only did the Egyptians consider a thick layer of eye paint beautiful, it also cut down on the sun's glare, like the black greasepaint today's football players sometimes wear under their eyes. In addition, the paint kept away flies and killed germs.

Many Egyptians shaved their heads and wore wigs. This probably kept them cooler and helped prevent lice. Men shaved their faces, too, but the pharaoh always wore a fake beard in public. The gods were often depicted with beards, and the fake beard symbolized the pharaoh's godlike status. Until the age of puberty, children's heads were often shaven except for one long piece of hair on the side.

HOUSE AND HOME

While pharaohs built huge palaces, most Egyptians lived in simple homes made of mud mixed with straw or sand to form bricks. Roofs were made of brick or wooden beams covered by reed mats and mud. Doors were made of papyrus. In the town of Kahun, the wealthy lived in mansions with up to 70 rooms, while pyramid workers' homes consisted of three to seven rooms measuring approximately 1,100 square feet (100 sq m).[1] In the worker village of Akhetaten, workers' homes contained four rooms, with a staircase leading to the roof or possibly to a second floor.

A wall surrounded all but the very poorest homes. Inside the courtyard, a small pond provided water for the surrounding plants. Roofed areas created shady spots to sit. Families often spent time on roof terraces under carefully placed awnings. Some terraces had scoop-shaped vents to catch breezes and provide a sort of natural air conditioning to the house. Farmhouses had stables and silos inside the walls.

The Egyptians painted the interior of their homes white and then added scenes from religion or nature. Rooms held furniture such as chairs, stools, beds, chests, or tables. Oil lamps provided light. Many families also built a small shrine to the gods in their homes. Wealthy families had small baths and toilets. These were simple seats made of limestone that had a hole in them. The waste collected in a container of sand that a slave would dispose of.

Egyptian Pets

Egyptians kept dogs and cats as pets. They also kept more unusual animals. Gazelles and monkeys were popular, as were geese. Pets often served a dual purpose—dogs might also act as guards, and dogs and cats both helped with hunting.

Cats held a special place in Egyptian society. The ancient people considered them sacred, and hurting a cat brought severe punishment, even death. Some people adorned their cats with earrings or other jewelry. The Egyptians mummified and buried their cats when they died.

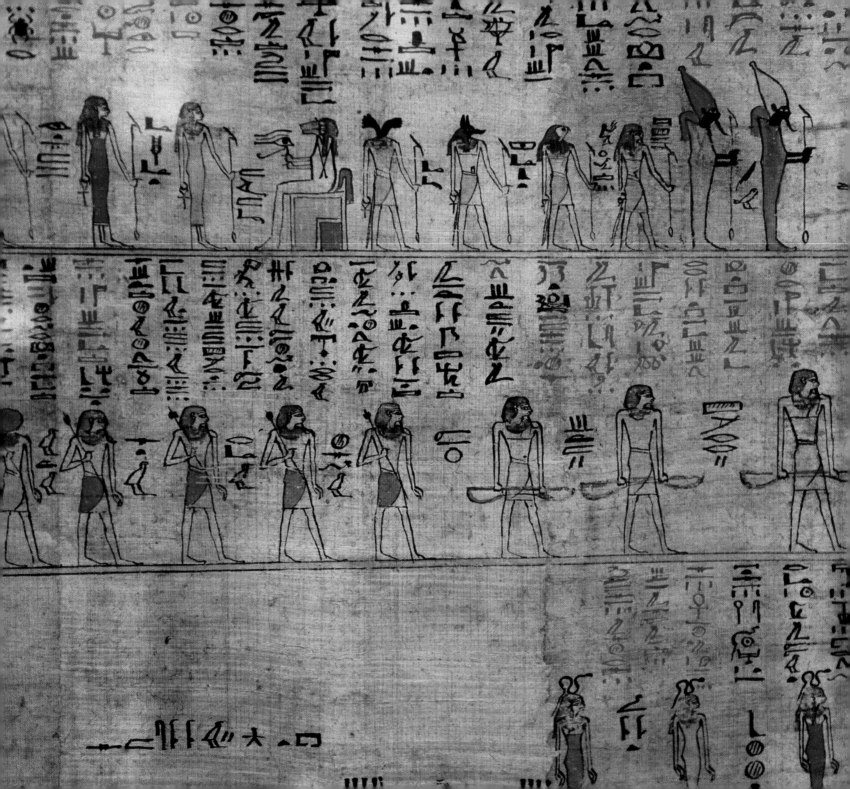

CHAPTER 5

WRITING AND ART

Writing was incredibly important and sacred to the Egyptians. They believed writing the name of a pharaoh gave him or her immortality, while destroying the written name killed the pharaoh forever.

A papyrus from the third intermediate period features a mixture of figures and hieroglyphics.

Egyptian scribes found plenty to write about. They wrote medical and religious texts and kept notes on court cases and battles. They also wrote lists, recipes, and stories. Scribes wrote on almost any available surface, including papyrus rolls, coffins, statues, temples, and walls.

Beginning in approximately 3500 BCE, the people of ancient Egypt wrote by pressing a tool into a clay tablet to form pictures called hieroglyphs. Clay was free. If it had not been baked, scribes could reuse the tablet by wetting the clay and rubbing out the letters. While this ability to make changes was beneficial, this early method also had a downside: the tablets could be quite large and heavy.

This early hieroglyphic script used symbols to represent both words and word sounds. For example, the symbol for the word *sun* was a circle with a tiny circle inside it. The symbol could also mean *day* or a phonetic sound from the Egyptian word for *sun*. However, the Egyptians never developed the symbols into an alphabet, and probably less than 5 percent of the population ever knew how to read the symbols.[1] Scribes used 600 to 700 hieroglyphs regularly. They used this type of writing mainly for religious texts. Today, scholars recognize approximately 6,000 signs.[2] Many of them are simply variations on the basic 600 to 700 signs from different regions or time periods.

In approximately 3000 BCE, the Egyptians figured out how to make papyrus from the papyrus reeds that grew in marshes near the Nile. The English word *paper* comes from *papyrus*. This process was a major step forward for the Egyptians.

Scribes used rush brushes and ink to write on papyrus. This new method of writing led to the development of a new style of script called *hieratic*, which developed around the same time as papyrus, approximately 2925. Hieratic also consisted of picture-like symbols, but they were simplified, like cursive writing is in English, and easier to write with flowing ink. Initially, the Egyptians wrote hieratic vertically. Later, they wrote it from right to left.

Papyrus

Papyrologists, scientists who study paper, have figured out how the ancient Egyptians probably made papyrus from the papyrus reed. The reed has a tough outer stem. The inner part of the reed is the pith. Papermakers cut the pith into the lengths desired for each page. They laid these pieces out in two layers that crisscrossed each other, one vertical and one horizontal. Next, they beat the stack of papyrus material with a mallet, pressed it overnight, and let it dry. After that, they polished the surface to smooth it, perhaps using a shell or piece of ivory, and the papyrus was ready to use. Sheets were joined into rolls. A typical roll contained 20 pages joined together with a type of glue, and rolls could be joined together. Archaeologists have found rolls as long as 132 feet (40 m).[3]

A CLOSER LOOK

THE ROSETTA STONE

Egyptian writing changed when the country officially converted to Christianity and, later, Islam. Eventually, people forgot how to read and write hieroglyphic script, and it became a lost language. For centuries, the secrets of the pyramids and ancient Egyptian life were lost to history. To scholars, Egyptian hieroglyphics were mysterious symbols. Some tried to decipher them, but no one was able to crack the code until the discovery of the Rosetta stone in 1799 CE.

That year, Napoléon Bonaparte was well on his way to conquering the world for France. During his expedition to Egypt, he set his soldiers to building a fort along the Nile Delta in a town formerly called Rosetta. There, they uncovered a huge slab of granite with inscriptions in hieroglyphic, demotic, and Greek. It measured approximately 44 inches (112 cm) long by 30 inches (76 cm) wide.[4] It weighed 1,680 pounds (762 kg).[5]

When the British defeated Napoléon in 1801 CE, they claimed the stone and placed it in the British Museum in London, England. Scholars realized it likely contained the same words written in all three languages. They were able to translate the ancient Greek text by 1803. The stone had been carved after the coronation of Ptolemy V in 196 BCE and praises the pharaoh and his accomplishments at length. Figuring out the hieroglyphic text would take much longer.

Finally, in 1822 CE, Jean-François Champollion cracked the code. The key to his discovery was that the hieroglyphs represented both words and word sounds for spelling other words. Experts used that knowledge to translate many other ancient Egyptian texts, and the study of Egyptology took off.

Scribes used hieratic for many purposes, from religious texts to business accounts and letters.

In approximately 650 BCE, the Egyptians developed a third script: *demotic*, which means "popular" or "of the people."[6] This was an even more simplified form of the hieratic script. They used it for business, legal, and literary writing for the next 1,000 years. The use of demotic did not mean the end of hieratic or the older hieroglyphic writing. Scribes continued to use hieratic for religious writing and hieroglyphic on stone carvings.

MUSIC AND BEAUTY

The Egyptians enjoyed music and dancing. Priests played instruments in the temples, and dancers performed at religious festivals and funerals. Musicians and dancers also entertained nobles in their homes and at banquets. Musicians played many types of instruments. Stringed varieties included the harp, the lute, and the lyre. Wind instruments were popular, including the double clarinet and double pipes, the flute, and the trumpet. Drums, the tambourine, and other shaken or rattled percussion instruments added rhythm.

The Egyptians appreciated beauty, and craftsmen created many beautiful items, some of which were also useful. Objects included jewelry, pottery, and mirrors. Artisans also produced pieces that are now famous, such as

Skilled artisans crafted this artifact from King Tut's tomb, a pendant of Nekhabet, the vulture goddess.

the bust of Nefertiti, which is on display in the Neues Museum in Berlin, Germany. Tomb paintings showed elaborate scenes from Egyptian life and the world of the gods. Large works of art were created by a team rather than an individual. Artists did not sign their work. Egyptians sometimes painted items such as pottery and furniture, usually with religious scenes.

GLASSMAKING

The ancient Egyptians created beautiful beads, figures, tiles, and other items from glass as early as 1250 BCE. To make the glass, they heated silica and ash to a high temperature, then crushed and washed the mixture before coloring it and melting it again. The molten glass was poured into molds to form chunks called ingots. These were later melted down again and shaped into their final form.

Artisans also formed clay into the desired shape and put it on the end of a metal rod. They built layers of glass over the clay, then removed the clay core. They worked with glass in other ways, too. One was to carve blocks of glass. Another was to pour molten glass into clay molds.

POTTERY

As early as 4750 BCE, Egyptians created vessels out of readily available clay. They developed so many styles over the years that archaeologists now use pottery types to date excavation sites.

To make pottery, the Egyptians kneaded clay by trampling it. They then added straw, chaff, or animal dung to make it less sticky. The potter shaped pots by hand or on a hand-turned potter's wheel. Next, he applied slip, which is clay thinned to a fine consistency, and often a wash of red ochre before drying and baking the pot. The first pots were probably baked on the

Faience animal figurines created by ancient Egyptian artists still maintain their distinctive blue color.

ground in a pile of fuel and animal dung. Later, potters used simple kilns. The Egyptians learned to glaze pottery in the 500s BCE.

Egyptian faience is a type of pottery. To make it, potters mixed crushed quartz or sand with a small amount of lime and ash, then added water to make a paste that could be shaped into jewelry and other decorative objects. They added a glaze before firing, often in a blue-green color. Potters made many small objects of faience, including amulets, beads, and ushabti.

CHAPTER 6

RULED BY GODS

In the beginning, the Egyptians believed, there was only the swirling, dark water of chaos, called Nun. Out of the water an island called Benben emerged, and on it stood the first god, Atum. Out of Atum's mouth came two other gods: Shu, the god of air, and Tefnut, the goddess of moisture. Soon, Shu and Tefnut had two children: Geb, the god of the earth, and Nut, the goddess of the sky. Shu placed Nut in an arch over Geb.

A carving at the Temple of Hatshepsut in Luxor, Egypt, depicts a pharaoh making offerings to the god Horus.

63

Nut and Geb had four children: Osiris, Isis, Seth, and Nephthys. Osiris and Isis became king and queen of the earth and ruled well. But Seth became jealous of Osiris and killed him. Osiris went to rule the underworld, and Seth became king of the earth. Seth ruled until Horus, the son of Osiris and Isis, killed him and became ruler of the earth in his place. Because Isis and Nephthys guarded Osiris's mummy, they became known as the guardians of coffins and canopic jars.

MANY GODS

Religion was everything to the ancient Egyptians. Because they lacked scientific understanding of the workings of the natural world, the ancient Egyptians believed the gods controlled things such as the journey of the sun across the sky each day and the flooding of the Nile. When the sun went down each evening, they feared it might not return. Priests prayed and made offerings to the gods to prevent such a terrible fate. At one point, the ancient Egyptians worshiped hundreds of gods. Many were connected with an animal.

One of the most important gods was Re, the sun god. He eventually merged with Amun, the god of the air and king of the gods, becoming Amun-Re. Others included those named in ancient Egypt's creation myth: Atum, Shu, Tefnut, Geb, Nut, Osiris, and Isis. The Egyptians believed their pharaohs were the god Horus, the son of Osiris and Isis, in human form. Thus, the pharaoh was the protector of the people, responsible for maintaining order and prosperity in both the human and the divine realms.

THE AFTERLIFE

Attaining eternal life was another important part of Egyptian religion. The Egyptians believed people were judged twice after death. First, their heart was placed on a scale with a feather on the other side. The feather stood for *ma'at*. Ma'at was also represented as a goddess. Osiris, king of the

Some Important Egyptian Gods

- Amun: god of the air and king of the gods

- Atum: the original god, who brought forth the world

- Geb: god of the earth

- Horus: the son of Osiris and Isis, he avenged his father's death and became king of the living, the earth, and the light

- Isis: the daughter of Geb and Nut as well as the sister and wife of Osiris, she became the supreme mother goddess

- Nut: goddess of the sky

- Osiris: the son of Geb and Nut, he became king of the underworld

- Re: god of the sun, he sailed across the sky each day and through the underworld at night

- Seth: son of Geb and Nut, he murdered his brother, Osiris

- Shu: god of the air

- Tefnut: goddess of moisture

underworld, presided over this process. Thoth, the god of writing, recorded and proclaimed the results. Earning eternal life depended entirely on doing no wrong. It did not matter whether one did anything good. If a person failed the test, his or her heart was tossed to Ammut, a monster with the head of a crocodile, the body of a lion, and the rear of a hippo, who gobbled it up. The Egyptians created the *Book of the Dead* to guide the deceased through this process.

Ancient Egyptians believed the soul had two parts: the *ba* and the *ka*. The ba represented the personality or character of a person and was shown as a bird with a human head. Family members left food by the tomb for the bird to eat until it left this world. The ka was the life force of the deceased. The two parts needed a place to reunite before traveling to the next world, which is why the Egyptians mummified their dead. Without a body, the person's soul could not journey on.

Initially, Egyptians buried their dead in the desert, placing them in tombs or coffins to prevent the sand from drying out the dead bodies. With time, the Egyptian burial ritual became more complex. Embalmers took 70 days to mummify a body. They used a salt called natron and various spices and oils and wrapped the body in linen. Embalmers were a class of priests. The priest who supervised the mummification process wore a mask in the form of a jackal to represent Anubis, the god of mummification.

MUMMIFICATION AND BURIAL

The ancient Egyptians showed great care in the process of mummification and burial. Embalming was a long and complicated task. Embalmers followed several steps in the 70–day process:

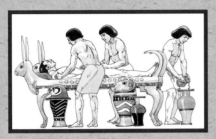

1. Remove the liver, stomach, intestines, and lungs and place them in four canopic jars. Pour fluid over them while prayers are offered. Leave the heart inside the body. Remove the brain through the nose with a long hook. Discard the brain.

2. Cover the body with natron, a mixture resembling baking soda and table salt. Dehydrating the body will take 40 days.

3. Wash the abdomen and chest cavities with wine and spices and pack them with resin-soaked linen. This holds the body in its original shape.

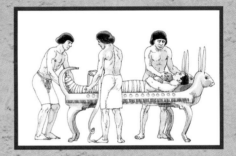

4. Anoint the body with oils, lotions, frankincense, and myrrh, creating a unique blend for each mummy.

5. Wrap the body with strips of linen and tuck in some amulets.

6. Place the body in a coffin inside a tomb with everything the deceased might need in the next life, including food, tools, clothing, and furniture.

7. Perform the Opening of the Mouth ritual and seal the tomb. Gather family and friends outside to share a memorial meal.

A CLOSER LOOK

THE *BOOK OF THE DEAD*

Originally, the Egyptians believed only pharaohs were guaranteed an afterlife. The secret spells buried with them, called the *Pyramid Texts*, were intended to help them make the journey to the next world safely. However, during the Middle Kingdom period, many of the pyramids were robbed, and the general public learned about the spells. They started putting them on their own coffins. These are known as the *Coffin Texts*. During the New Kingdom, many of the spells from the *Pyramid Texts* and *Coffin Texts* were written on papyrus scrolls and tucked into coffins. These scrolls, known as the *Book of the Dead*, made up a sort of travel guide to the underworld.

The *Book of the Dead* included spells, prayers, songs, and rituals to help deceased people in their journey to the next world. It named the 42 judging gods in order to give a person more power over them. It also spelled out ways for deceased people to convince the gods they were innocent of wrongdoing. For example, a person might say, "Hail, Strider, coming forth from Heliopolis, I have done no wrong."[1] If he or she were judged "true of voice," that person would be allowed to pass through to the underworld.[2]

Each copy of the *Book of the Dead* was slightly different, and wealthier people could have theirs personalized with their name and chosen spells. Numerous examples are available in museums around the world. The longest is the "Greenfield Papyrus," currently on display at the British Museum in London.

After embalming, priests performed the Opening of the Mouth ritual. This series of words and motions was thought to magically open the person's mouth, eyes, and ears so they would work in the afterlife. The living placed a copy of the *Book of the Dead* in the coffin or wrote its texts on the tomb walls. The deceased people could consult the book's spells and instructions in their journey to the afterlife. The Egyptians also placed ushabti in tombs. These small figurines represented servants, who would work for the deceased person in the afterlife. The Egyptians mummified pets and sacred animals and sometimes placed the creatures with their owners as well.

TEMPLES AND WORSHIP

Because the gods had to be kept happy so Egypt would function well, the pharaohs built temples to many gods. These temples grew larger and more impressive over time. During the reign of Ramses III, the temple complex at Karnak employed more than 80,000 people.[3] Farmers, carpenters, jewelers, and scribes were among those who worked there. Some temples served as centers of learning, where students came to study astronomy, astrology, and religion. Some temples contained libraries.

A statue of the god for whom a temple had been built sat in its inner chamber. Priests entered the inner chamber each day to feed, dress, and apply cosmetics and perfumes to the temple statue. On special festival days, the Egyptians took the statue out of the temple and paraded it in public. Priests, people, or boats carried the statue in public.

Egyptian priests and priestesses made prayers and offerings to the gods to keep them happy. For the most part, priests dealt only with big issues, such as making the sun rise and the Nile flood. Although ordinary people could not enter the temple, they often built small shrines to hold household gods. In some cases, they could say prayers into the ears of the god through paintings on the outer wall of a temple.

In the earliest times, the pharaoh served as high priest, traveling to each temple. However, as the population and the number of temples grew, he did not have time to do this all on his own.

Remains of the temple at Karnak, Egypt, still tower today.

He appointed priests to help. Usually, these were members of the royal family. Priests often had regular jobs as craftsmen or scribes as well and served in their temple for only one month per year.

MAGIC AND MEDICINE

Magic and medicine blurred together in ancient Egypt. People went to temples for healing. And doctors were specialized priests. For the most part, if doctors could see and identify a person's problem, they used medicine. If not, they used magic. Magic treatments included spells and special acts or gestures. Many Egyptians wore amulets to ward off illness. The Egyptians also used magic to protect against dangers, demons, and enemies. For instance, they tried to protect themselves from Nile crocodiles by pointing the index and little fingers of one hand at them.

The Egyptians had a fairly good idea of internal anatomy through mummification, but it was far from complete or accurate. They thought the heart held the emotions and intellect, and they saw little need for the brain. Still, they could set broken bones, amputate limbs, and even create prosthetic limbs. They knew how to use bandages, splints, and compresses. Archaeologists have found samples of ancient medical tools, along with scrolls containing medical lectures and instructions for surgeons. One of these, the "Edwin Smith Papyrus," dates to approximately 1600 BCE and is likely a copy of another manuscript, perhaps from 3000 BCE. The papyrus lists symptoms and remedies for common medical problems.

Ancient Egyptians had other remedies for healing. For example, they consumed pomegranate root or the wormwood plant to get rid of parasitic worms. The honey and propolis the Egyptians often put on open wounds are now known to kill bacteria. However, other remedies would have been useless at best or even harmful.

While the Egyptians thought of themselves as a strong and vigorous people, most mummies show signs of infection by at least one parasite. Desert lung disease and black lung disease were epidemic, and diseases such as malaria, smallpox, and tuberculosis probably affected many Egyptians.

Mummies Unwrapped

Humans have long had a fascination with mummies, and they star in many scary stories. In the 1800s CE, some wealthy Europeans imported mummies and hosted mummy-unwrapping parties to create a spooky experience for their guests. Scientists unwrapped mummies to study their bodies. Today, X ray and CT scan technologies allow scientists to study mummies without unwrapping them or even opening their coffins. These medical techniques provide clues to the mummy's identity and cause of death. Researchers can even reconstruct faces to see what the person looked like in life.

CHAPTER 7

CRAFTING PYRAMIDS

"Man fears time, but time fears the pyramids," says an old Arabic proverb.[1] Perhaps more than any other artifact, these timeless monuments capture the essence and the mystery of this remarkable civilization.

The Pyramids of Giza are a lasting testament to the building skills of the ancient Egyptians.

The first Egyptian royal tombs were low, rectangular buildings called mastabas built in the desert at Abydos. The art and craft of pyramid building peaked during the Old Kingdom with the construction of the Great Pyramids of Giza. These three pyramids are part of a chain of pyramids that stretch for almost 20 miles (32 km) along the edge of the desert west of the Nile. Archaeologists have discovered 138 pyramids in Egypt so far. The Egyptians crafted these mighty structures with simple hand tools—stone hammers, copper picks and chisels, and wooden levers.

The largest of all the Pyramids, the Great Pyramid, covers 13 acres (5 ha) of land. The square base is 756 feet (230 m) on a side. The pyramid originally stood 481 feet (147 m) high and is now 451 feet (137 m) because thieves stripped off its limestone casing in ancient times.[2] Khafre's and Menkaure's pyramids nearby were slightly smaller.

The Great Pyramid contains 2.3 million stone blocks. Each one weighs an average of 2.5 short tons (2.3 metric tons).[3] Scholars estimate more than 20,000 men worked to build the Great Pyramid, placing an average of one block every two minutes, ten hours per day, for 20 years.[4]

Workers cut stones from the quarries and hauled them to the pyramid on sleds, which worked better on the desert sand than wheeled vehicles. Men or oxen pulled the sleds.

Building the Pyramids required precise measurements, and the Egyptians' excellent practical skills in arithmetic, measurement, and geometry allowed them to plan and erect these massive monuments with blocks that fit together with the utmost precision.

THE PYRAMID BUILDERS

Historians once thought slaves built the Pyramids. More recent evidence tells a different story. Instead of slaves, skilled builders and craftsmen lived in the towns specially constructed near the Pyramids. Peasant farmers came and worked for several months each year in exchange for food and supplies, usually during the inundation, when their fields were flooded.

The work was hard and dangerous. Bones found in a cemetery near Giza show that, like other peasants, most pyramid builders died between the ages of 35 and 40. The builders' skeletons show degenerative joint diseases, amputations, and fractured skulls and limbs.

Pyramid construction crews labored until sundown each day. The workmen got one day off every ten days. On occasional feast days, they

Pyramids Past

Today, the Giza Pyramids look like rough, worn piles of stones. When they were built, the Pyramids looked very different. The outside was covered with smooth, angled casing stones that gleamed white in the sun and moonlight. These stones were stripped off for use as building material in the nearby city of Cairo sometime between the 1100s and 1800s CE.

Building pyramids required many men working together.

could visit their families. Although Egyptians celebrated as many as 100 feast days each year, the builders likely did not stop work for most of them. The craftsmen and overseers worked a less grueling schedule.

Researchers experimented to see how difficult it would be for workers to drag the heavy pyramid stones up a ramp. They found that 10 to 12 men could drag a massive stone with ropes, using water to wet the ramp.[5] They believe the Egyptians dragged the stones for the Great Pyramid over a long ramp to the building and up a spiral ramp around the outside—or possibly inside—of the pyramid.

Builders cut pyramid stones from huge quarries using flint chisels and wooden mallets. To cut the stones, they made a groove, poured sand in it, and rubbed the sand with a toothless copper saw to form a cut. The strongest tools available during the Old Kingdom were made of copper, so both the Great Sphinx and the Great Pyramid were built with only copper and stone tools. Highly skilled masons used these tools to carve the relatively soft limestone and harder granite and diorite. To place the stones, builders used plumb bobs, cubits, squares, measuring lines, and leveling staffs. Ramps, sledges, rollers, ropes, and levers helped workers lift and move the heavy rock, creating the magnificent structures that have survived for millennia.

METALLURGY

The ancient Egyptians began metallurgy, specifically copper, in approximately 3000 BCE. They mined copper ore from the eastern deserts. They learned to harden the metal by heating it to a high temperature, cooling it, and then hammering it. At first, they poured the copper into a flat sheet that was bent or pounded into the shape desired. They later learned to pour the metal into molds to create desired shapes and to make hollow objects using a clay core.

Next, the Egyptians discovered how to mix tin with the copper to make bronze. Bronze is harder than tin and copper and easier to shape and cast. They used bronze to make temple doors, pots, tools, and weapons.

The first iron ore came from meteorites, and the world's oldest-known iron artifacts are 5,000-year-old Egyptian beads made from this material. Smelting iron required extremely high temperatures. The Egyptians began manufacturing iron between 1000 and 600 BCE with more sophisticated techniques they likely learned from neighboring countries. All these

Learning about the Pyramid Builders

Much of the knowledge about the lives of the pyramid builders comes from the excavation of the towns where they lived. Kahun was the first of these ever discovered. It housed the workers who built the Pyramid at Al-Lahun for the pharaoh Senusret II in approximately 1895 BCE. The man responsible for its excavation in the late 1800s CE is one of the most important Egyptologists: Sir William Matthew Flinders Petrie.

Sometimes called the "father of archaeology," Petrie was almost completely self-taught.[6] He was an excellent mathematician, photographer, and surveyor, and he almost single-handedly made archaeology into the science it is today.

A careful observer, Petrie studied the pottery he found at excavation sites and classified it into various categories. He used his classification system to help date the finds at each level of the dig site, a process now known as seriation. Archaeologists still use this method of systematic excavation.

improvements in metalworking technology bettered the Egyptians' lives by providing them with stronger, more effective tools.

BOATBUILDING

The Egyptians started building boats as early as 6,000 years ago. Living along the Nile, they relied on boats for transportation. Flat barges hauled stones to building sites. Ferries carried people across the river. People used boats for pleasure trips and fishing. Because the prevailing winds blow in the opposite direction as the Nile's current flows, boats could easily sail upstream and float downstream. Oars sped up the process. Within the delta region, small boats navigated the maze of rivers, streams, and marshes.

Few trees grew in Egypt, so the Egyptians first made boats by binding papyrus reeds together. Later, the Egyptians used cedar from Lebanon or pine from Syria, joining planks with ropes threaded through holes.

Archaeologists have discovered some good examples of ancient Egyptian boats. One artifact was a complete boat, in pieces, buried near the Great Pyramid in Giza, presumably intended to carry the pharaoh on his journey to the underworld. The boat was sealed in a large pit that preserved it for approximately 4,000 years. Scholars worked for years to fit its 1,224 pieces together like a giant jigsaw puzzle.[7]

CHAPTER 8

ESTABLISHING AN EMPIRE

Scholars have learned much about the ancient Egyptians through their paintings and carvings on temple walls, including the civilization's military adventures. Most wars were fought over territory, either defending it or, in later years, extending it. Ancient Egyptians had several advantages when it came to defending their land. Wide deserts stretched

A painted box from King Tut's tomb shows the pharaoh at war, fighting Syrians with arrows from his chariot.

out on the east and west, making it difficult for invaders to approach from those directions. The Nile's marshy delta to the north and the huge boulders and rapids to the south of Egypt made entering from either direction difficult for ships. With few threats from their neighbors and productive land that provided for their needs, the early Egyptians did not need to conquer other lands. The army was mainly used for practical purposes, such as guarding palaces, borders, and shipments from the mines.

Occasional skirmishes were a way of life—the Egyptians frequently raided Nubia to seize gold. Narmer, the first pharaoh of united Egypt, may have been the first to lead Egyptian armies into other lands. In 1994 CE, archaeologists working in Israel unearthed a pottery shard with his name on it. When Egyptian forces fought, the pharaoh always led his troops in battle. Many times, however, the Egyptians hired mercenaries, or foreign soldiers, to fight abroad for them because they were afraid of dying far from home without a proper burial to help them to the afterlife.

After the Hyksos invaded Egypt during the second intermediate period, the pharaohs realized they needed to control their neighbors. The Egyptian leaders formed a professional army and began establishing an empire.

WEAPONS

Ancient Egyptian warriors fought with maces, spears, and swords in open territory. When enemy troops started wearing metal helmets, the Egyptians started carrying battle-axes. They also fought with straight and curved swords.

Meanwhile, archers rained arrows on the enemy. Early bows were made of acacia wood. Later, stronger composite bows were made of animal horn, tendons, and wood. With these, archers could shoot an arrow up to 1,500 feet (457 m). The Egyptians used reeds or wood to make their arrow shafts and tipped them with flint, ivory, or metal arrowheads.

Other warriors tossed javelins, which were long wooden shafts with metal tips. Slingshots, originally used to protect herds of animals from predators, were made from a piece of leather with a string on each end and were used to fling stones at the enemy.

Egyptian soldiers carried shields to protect themselves against spears, swords, and daggers. Shields were made of leather or wood and sometimes were covered with metal. Sometimes, soldiers wore body armor in the form

"When the sun shone forth on the land, I was upon him like a falcon. When the time for perfuming the mouth [lunch] came, I defeated him, I destroyed his wall, I killed his people. . . . My soldiers were like lions upon their prey, carrying off slaves, cattle, fat, and honey, and dividing their possessions."[1]

—Kamose, a prince of Thebes, boasting of driving out the Hyksos during the second intermediate period of a leather apron, which they wore over a kilt. They probably did not wear helmets until the late period and then mainly while driving chariots.

The Egyptians' simple weapons worked well for 700 years, until the Hyksos invaded. These people came from the north and conquered Lower Egypt. Scholars are unsure whether their takeover was peaceful or violent. Regardless, they would rule for more than a century during the second intermediate period. By the end of that time, they used horses and chariots to subdue the Egyptians, who likely had never seen horses before. The Hyksos may have also brought composite bows to Egypt.

The Egyptians quickly learned to use chariots and horses in war. Two horses pulled the chariot. The driver steered while his partner held up a shield and launched his weapons.

SOLDIERS

Egypt's first armies likely consisted of farmers who either volunteered during the inundation or were drafted. As motivation to join, soldiers received a share of the booty they captured. This system

Adopting the Chariot

The Egyptians do not appear to have used wheels until the Hyksos introduced chariots during the second intermediate period. The Egyptians soon improved chariot design by adding additional spokes to the wheels, making them stronger. Chariots became a status symbol. Artists often depicted pharaohs driving them alone, with the reins tied around their waists—a possible but rather unlikely feat.

Chariots carried soldiers, and they were also weapons because they could crush the enemy.

lasted approximately 1,500 years. By the beginning of the New Kingdom, in approximately 1500 BCE, full-time soldiers took over, although men could still be drafted if needed. The military organized its foot soldiers into divisions of 5,000 men.[2] Companies had 200 men and platoons had 50 men.[3]

Military life was harsh, offering meager rations, frequent beatings, and little opportunity for advancement. Soldiers had to forage and steal to get enough to eat. They marched approximately 15 miles (24 km) a day carrying a pack and a staff or a club.[4] Soldiers received weapons when they were ready to attack the enemy, which they did barefoot.

FORTRESSES

The Egyptians built large fortresses on their borders and smaller forts in the desert hills. While geography protected much of the country, Egypt was vulnerable along its borders with Nubia, Palestine, and Libya. These areas required extra protection.

Fortresses along the Nubian border are the best studied because some of their ruins still stand. Built on high peaks along the Nile, they were surrounded by extremely thick walls that often were encircled by more walls and ditches. Sentries in watchtowers kept a lookout. Fortresses guarded Egypt's borders and protected its trade routes.

FOREIGN INVASIONS

While ancient Egypt remained relatively stable for its 3,000-year existence, the ancient civilization did not go without

An ancient Egyptian carving captures soldiers fighting on a ladder.

being attacked. Other nations attempted to invade it from time to time. The Egyptians fought off many of them but not all. The first successful invaders were the Hyksos, whose superior weapons allowed them to rule Egypt for approximately a century before the princes of Thebes overthrew them in 1567 BCE.

The next invasion took place in 664 BCE, when the Assyrians seized control and set up their own rulers. The Persians followed in 525 BCE. They conquered Egypt as far as Memphis in the north, making it part of the Persian Empire.

Less than 200 years later, Alexander the Great, a Greek king, invaded Egypt. When he died, the commanders in his army divided up the conquered lands. Ptolemy I became pharaoh of Egypt, beginning a line of Ptolemaic pharaohs. In 51 BCE, Ptolemy XII's daughter, Cleopatra VII, took power. She was the last to rule before Egypt fell to the Roman Emperor Augustus in 30 BCE and became part of the Roman Empire.

The Navy

During the New Kingdom, the Egyptian Navy played an active role in military expeditions, especially when Egyptians were fighting abroad and establishing an empire. Before that time, the navy primarily transported troops. The ancient Egyptians built their first warships during the New Kingdom. These ships measured up to 200 feet (61 m) long.[5] They had a row of oars on each side to move the boat through the water.

CHAPTER 9

THE LEGACY OF ANCIENT EGYPT

Today, Egypt is a modern, high-tech nation that in some ways bears little resemblance to the land of the pharaohs. With gleaming steel bridges, huge dams, and towering skyscrapers, its cities look much like other bustling metropolises. Yet, all this activity is set against the backdrop of the Pyramids, Great Sphinx,

The Great Sphinx has become an icon of ancient Egypt.

temples, and tombs—a silent but ever-present reminder of the country's rich history and legacy.

As the only surviving example of the Seven Wonders of the Ancient World, the Giza Pyramids, along with the many other pyramids and monuments in Egypt, continue to amaze and inspire those who see them. The Egyptian Museum in Cairo houses a huge collection of ancient Egyptian artifacts, including items from King Tut's tomb. Visitors travel from all over the world to view and study them.

THE LESSONS OF ANCIENT EGYPT

Studying ancient Egypt reveals much about human history because the civilization is so well preserved. Not only is Egypt's climate ideal for preserving bodies and artifacts, but the ancient Egyptians' religious beliefs caused them to preserve items and bodies very carefully.

One exciting development in Egyptology is the rapidly growing field of paleopathology, which is the study of ancient disease. By studying mummies, scientists can learn much about the evolution and history of disease. Paleopathology relies on scientific techniques such as DNA analysis, X rays, and CT scans to study Egyptian mummies. Because mummy tissue samples remain intact along with the bones, scientists can learn new details about the health and genetics of the mummified Egyptians. The modern population of Egypt is genetically similar, so scientists can trace the history of various diseases over millennia.

By examining mummies, scientists can learn how they died and much about how they lived. As Egyptologist Zahi Hawass wrote in *National Geographic* magazine, "Mummies capture our imaginations and our hearts. Full of secrets and magic, they were once people who lived and loved, just as we do today."[1] Mummies and artifacts can teach people today much about ancient Egypt and, ultimately, about themselves.

Studies of hieroglyphic inscriptions on tombs and papyrus continue to shed light on Egyptian history and culture, from the glories of battle to death

The Pharos of Alexandria

Egypt was once home to another wonder of the ancient world. For centuries, the Lighthouse of Alexandria, called the Pharos because it was on the island of Pharos, lighted the way for sailors approaching the coast of Egypt. Completed in approximately 280 BCE, the lighthouse stood more than 350 feet (110 m) tall.[2] People as far as 25 miles (40 km) away could see its light.[3]

A special system of mirrors reflected fires burning inside. The Pharos fell into ruins by the 1100s CE due to a series of earthquakes. In 1477, the remaining material was used to build a fort at the same site. In the 1900s, archaeologists working underwater discovered a treasure trove of artifacts at the site of the Pharos, including columns, sphinxes, statues, and huge blocks of granite.

to taxes. And ancient Egyptian tools and everyday items give us a snapshot of human history as they progressed from stone to copper to bronze to iron and steel and beyond.

EGYPTIAN INFLUENCE SPREADS

Ancient Egypt's accomplishments influenced the rest of the world in concrete ways. Egyptian doctors laid the foundation for modern medicine. They were pioneers in the fields of anatomy, surgery, and pharmacy. They were the first to use bandages, splints, and compresses. In later years, the Greeks went to Alexandria to practice dissection and carried many Egyptian ideas back with them to Greece.

Egyptians led the world in practical mathematics as well. They figured out clever tricks for multiplication, subtraction, fractions, and measurement. They were also masters of geometry, having figured out how to build incredibly complex monuments and pyramids. Many famous Greek mathematicians may have studied in Egypt, including Pythagoras, Plato, Archimedes, and Thales.

Egyptian architecture gave the world the obelisk and the pyramid, which have inspired architects in many other eras and cultures, including the United States. The Egyptians also invented accurate calendar and timekeeping systems, even without understanding how the earth orbits the sun. But perhaps one of their most important inventions was writing on papyrus. This precursor to paper allowed language and literature to be easily and inexpensively shared with the world. However, it was expensive enough to limit its use to religious and important secular documents.

REDISCOVERING EGYPT

When Napoléon invaded Egypt in 1798, he took along 167 scientists and technicians who spent three years mapping the country and studying its ecology, irrigation systems, customs, monuments, and artifacts.[6] This group published its results and brought many specimens and antiquities back to Europe, sparking a passionate interest in Egyptology. Wealthy travelers began conducting excavations

Uses for Mummies

Over the centuries, people have treated mummies with shocking disrespect. During the Middle Ages, doctors ground them up to use as medicine for fractures, concussions, coughs, nausea, ulcers, and more. Mummy medicines were so popular that exporters started making fake mummies from recently executed criminals and people who committed suicide to meet the demand. And artists ground them up to make "Mummy Brown" pigment. Today, archaeologists handle mummies with great respect and disturb them as little as possible.

New Tools for Exploration

One of the most exciting technologies in archaeology is ground-penetrating radar (GPR). Archaeologists previously had to dig almost at random to look for buried archaeological features. Now, using GPR, they can create maps of underground features by simply running a radar device over the area. The GPR unit sends out radar waves that bounce off buried objects or changes in soil and are received by an antenna to create a 3-D map. In recent decades, scientists have found multiple tombs and mummies using GPR.

to add to their collections. Unfortunately, they removed many important artifacts from their original locations without proper documentation. Treasure hunting, rather than archaeology, was the name of the game.

Slowly, excavations became more scientific, and Egypt established its Antiquities Ministry in the 1850s to safeguard its archaeological treasures. Today, researchers conduct excavations scientifically to disturb the artifacts as little as possible and learn about each item in its original context. Much more remains to be learned through Egyptology. As scientists continue to study all that the people of ancient Egypt learned, lived, and did, one thing is certain: just as they have for millennia, the Pyramids will still stand as a silent testimony to the glories and struggles of ancient Egypt and will continue to inspire the world.

The temples built by Ramses II at Abu Simbel are among the numerous creations of ancient Egypt that have stood the test of time and draw visitors today.

TIMELINE

C. 5000–2926 BCE
During the predynastic period, Egyptians create small kingdoms along the Nile valley.

2925 BCE
Narmer unites Upper and Lower Egypt and becomes unified Egypt's first ruler.

2925–2575 BCE
The early dynastic period marks the beginning of ancient Egyptian history.

2575–2130 BCE
The pharaohs have great power and build massive monuments during the Old Kingdom.

C. 2550 BCE
The Egyptians build the Great Pyramid of Giza.

C. 2520 BCE
The Egyptians build the Great Sphinx at Giza.

2269–2175 BCE
Pepi II reigns for 94 years.

2130–1938 BCE
The first intermediate period, a time of great upheaval and chaos, occurs.

1938–1630 BCE
The Middle Kingdom period is a time of prosperity.

1630–1540 BCE
The pharaohs lose control of the country, and chaos ensues during the second intermediate period.

1630–1523 BCE
The Hyksos invade and rule Egypt.

1539–1075 BCE
Egypt unites again and dominates many of its neighbors during the New Kingdom period.

1353–1336 BCE
Amenhotep IV tries to get rid of all but one god.

1333–1323 BCE
Tutankhamen reigns and restores the old gods.

1279–1213 BCE
Ramses II rules and builds many great monuments.

1075–656 BCE
The kingdom is divided during the third intermediate period.

664–332 BCE
Persian kings rule the country during the late period.

332 BCE
Alexander the Great conquers Egypt.

30 BCE
Egypt falls to Rome and becomes part of the Roman Empire.

391 CE
The arrival of Christianity brings an end to ancient Egyptian culture.

ANCIENT HISTORY

KEY DATES

- 2925–2575 BCE: early dynastic period

- 2575–2130 BCE: Old Kingdom

- 1938–1630 BCE: Middle Kingdom

- 1539–1075 BCE: New Kingdom

- 664–332 BCE: late period

KEY TOOLS AND TECHNOLOGY

- The Egyptians learned to make copper, bronze, and iron tools that helped them build everything from household furniture to weapons to huge statues and pyramids.

- Their skill in practical mathematics let them create accurate calendars and tell time.

- They made great advances in medicine, learning to set broken bones, dress wounds, and treat common illnesses using herbal and mineral remedies.

- They recorded their history, religion, and legal and financial information first on pottery and stone and later on papyrus, a precursor to paper the Egyptians invented.

LANGUAGES

Beginning in approximately 3500 BCE, the Egyptians wrote using pictures called hieroglyphs. They developed hieratic, a cursive style of writing, in approximately 2925 BCE. In approximately 650 BCE, the Egyptians developed an even more simplified script: demotic. Scribes used it for business, legal, and literary writing for the next thousand years. They also continued using hieratic for religious writings and hieroglyphic on stone carvings. Ancient written Egyptian eventually became a dead language. No one could read it until the Rosetta stone was deciphered in 1822 CE.

EVOLUTION OF THE PYRAMID

- Mastaba: popular in 2630 BCE, when Djoser had one built for his burial

- Step Pyramid: Djoser's style of mastaba developed into a step pyramid by 2611 BCE with the addition of five mastabas stacked on top of the first

- Khufu's Great Pyramid: built in approximately 2500 BCE, the steps of previous pyramids evolved into smooth sides

IMPACT OF THE EGYPTIAN CIVILIZATION

- Egyptian medicine, mathematics, and architecture—including the obelisk and pyramid—influenced the Greeks and other European cultures and laid the foundation for much of what people know about these subjects today.

- The Egyptian practice of mummifying their dead and building tombs—together with the warm, dry climate—preserved many priceless artifacts. Egyptologists continue to study Egyptian art, music, history, culture, and language to learn more about human history and how these ancient people lived. One of the most exciting lines of study is paleopathology, the study of ancient disease. By examining mummies, scientists can learn how they died and much about how they lived.

QUOTE

"Mummies capture our imaginations and our hearts. Full of secrets and magic, they were once people who lived and loved, just as we do today."

—*Zahi Hawass, Egyptian archaeologist, Egyptologist, and former director of Egypt's Ministry of Antiquities*

GLOSSARY

canopic jar
A stone or pottery jar used for holding the internal organs of a mummified person.

capstone
The finishing stone of a structure.

cubit
A measure of length based on the length of the forearm, usually 17 to 21 inches (43 to 53 cm).

dynasty
A family that controls a country for a long period of time through successive rulers.

embalm
To preserve a dead body.

flail
A long-handled tool used to beat wheat so the grain would become separated from the ear.

hieratic
A simplified form of hieroglyphics used in ancient Egypt.

loincloth
A piece of material worn around the hips.

ma'at
A principle of truth, justice, order, and harmony in the universe and in Egypt, represented by the goddess Ma'at.

metallurgy
The science of metalworking.

natron
A natural sodium carbonate and sodium bicarbonate mixture used for drying out bodies in the mummification process.

ochre
A mixture of iron oxide and earth that forms a pigment.

oryx
A large African antelope with long, straight horns.

plumb bob
A weight at the end of a string used in construction.

propolis
A waxy material bees collect from trees and use as a cement in hives.

vizier
An adviser to the pharaoh.

ADDITIONAL RESOURCES

SELECTED BIBLIOGRAPHY

David, Rosalie, and Rick Archbold. *Conversations with Mummies: New Light on the Lives of the Ancient Egyptians*. New York: William Morrow, 2000. Print.

Erlich, Haggai, and Israel Gershoni. *The Nile: Histories, Cultures, Myths*. Boulder, CO: Lynne Rienner, 1999. Print.

Redford, Donald B., ed. *The Oxford Encyclopedia of Ancient Egypt, v. 1–3*. New York: Oxford UP, 2000. Print.

Smith, Craig B. *How the Great Pyramid Was Built*. Washington, DC: Smithsonian, 2004. Print.

FURTHER READINGS

Kallen, Stuart A. *Understanding World History: Ancient Egypt*. San Diego, CA: ReferencePoint, 2011. Print.

Pocket Genius: Ancient Egypt. Facts at Your Fingertips. New York: DK Children, 2012. Print.

Yomtov, Nel. *The Ancient World: Ancient Egypt*. New York: Scholastic, 2012. Print.

WEBSITES

To learn more about Ancient Civilizations, visit **booklinks.abdopublishing.com**. These links are routinely monitored and updated to provide the most current information available.

PLACES TO VISIT

BRITISH MUSEUM

British Museum, Great Russell Street

London, WC1B 3DG

44-0-20-7323-8000

http://www.britishmuseum.org

This museum holds the largest and most comprehensive collection of ancient Egyptian art and artifacts outside Cairo, Egypt, including the Rosetta stone, a gallery of monumental sculptures (containing a statue of Ramses II), and an impressive display of mummies and coffins.

EGYPTIAN MUSEUM

Midan El Tahrir

Cairo, Egypt 11557

202-5782448

http://www.emuseum.gov.eg

This museum features a Tutankhamen collection and the Royal Mummy Room.

MUSEUM OF FINE ARTS

465 Huntington Avenue

Boston, Massachusetts 02115

617-267-9300

http://www.mfa.org

The museum's Egyptian collection has more than 40,000 items, including a collection of ancient artifacts.

SOURCE NOTES

Chapter 1. Fertile Soil

1. "Tutankhamun (1336 BC–1327 BC)." *BBC*. BBC, 2014. Web. 17 Sept. 2014.

2. Toby Wilkinson. *The Rise and Fall of Ancient Egypt*. New York: Random, 2010. Print. 15.

3. David P. Silverman, ed. *Ancient Egypt*. New York: Oxford UP, 1997. Print. 10.

4. "Geography." *Ancient Egypt*. British Museum, 2014. Web. 17 Sept. 2014.

5. David P. Silverman, ed. *Ancient Egypt*. New York: Oxford UP, 1997. Print. 7.

6. Howard Carter. *The Tomb of Tutankhamen*. London, UK: Little, 2007. Print. 51.

7. "Howard Carter, 64, Egyptologist, Dies." *New York Times*. New York Times, 3 Mar. 1939. Web. 17 Sept. 2014.

Chapter 2. Thriving in a Desert

1. Susan Wise Baurer. *The History of the Ancient World: From the Earliest Accounts to the Fall of Rome*. New York: Norton. Print. 26.

2. Toby Wilkinson. *The Rise and Fall of Ancient Egypt*. New York: Random, 2010. Print. 57.

3. Alan H. Gardiner. *The Admonitions of an Egyptian Sage from a Hieratic Papyrus in Leiden*. Leipzig, Germany: Georg Olms Verlag, 1969. 9. *Google Book Search*. Web. 17 Sept. 2014.

4. David P. Silverman, ed. *Ancient Egypt*. New York: Oxford UP, 1997. Print. 31.

5. Bob Brier and Hoyt Hobbs. *Ancient Egypt: Everyday Life in the Land of the Nile*. New York: Sterling, 2009. Print. 26.

Chapter 3. Kings, Classes, and Commerce

1. Margaret R. Bunson. *Encyclopedia of Ancient Egypt*. New York: Facts on File, 2002. Print. 161–162.
2. Bob Brier and Hoyt Hobbs. *Ancient Egypt: Everyday Life in the Land of the Nile*. New York: Sterling, 2009. Print. 78.
3. "Pharaoh." Encyclopædia Britannica. Encyclopædia Britannica, 2014. Web. 17 Sept. 2014.
4. Rosalie David. *Handbook to Life in Ancient Egypt*. New York: Facts on File, 2003. Print. 202.
5. Toby Wilkinson. *The Rise and Fall of Ancient Egypt*. New York: Random, 2010. Print. 255.
6. Bob Brier and Hoyt Hobbs. *Ancient Egypt: Everyday Life in the Land of the Nile*. New York: Sterling, 2009. Print. 90.

Chapter 4. A Day in the Life

1. David P. Silverman, ed. *Ancient Egypt*. New York: Oxford UP, 1997. Print. 71–72.

Chapter 5. Writing and Art

1. Rosalie David and Rick Archbold. *Conversations with Mummies*. New York: HarperCollins/Madison, 2000. Print. 32.
2. David P. Silverman, ed. *Ancient Egypt*. New York: Oxford UP, 1997. Print. 232.
3. Hans Arne Jensen. *Plant World of the Bible*. Bloomington, IN: AuthorHouse, 2013. *Google Book Search*. Web. 17 Sept. 2014.
4. "The Rosetta Stone." *BritishMuseum.org*. British Museum, n.d. Web. 17 Sept. 2014.
5. Lawrence Van Gelder. "Arts, Briefly." *New York Times*. New York Times, 1 May 2007. Web. 17 Sept. 2014.
6. "Demotic." *Online Etymology Dictionary*. Douglas Harper, 2014. Web. 17 Sept. 2014.

Chapter 6. Ruled by Gods

1. Pat Remler. "Judgment Day in Egyptian Mythology." *Egyptian Mythology A to Z*. Mythology A to Z. New York: Facts on File, 2006. *Ancient and Medieval History Online*. Facts on File, n.d. Web. 17 Sept. 2014.
2. Ibid.
3. Rosalie David. *Handbook to Life in Ancient Egypt*. New York: Facts on File, 2003. Print. 159.

SOURCE NOTES CONTINUED

Chapter 7. Crafting Pyramids

1. Toby Wilkinson. *The Rise and Fall of Ancient Egypt*. New York: Random, 2010. Print. 75.

2. "Pyramids of Giza." Encyclopædia Britannica. Encyclopædia Britannica, 2014. Web. 17 Sept. 2014.

3. "Great Pyramid: Earth's Largest." *National Geographic*. National Geographic Society, 1996. Web. 17 Sept. 2014.

4. Zahi Hawass. *Mountains of the Pharaohs*. New York: Doubleday, 2006. Print. 159.

5. Ibid. 62.

6. Rosalie David. *Handbook to Life in Ancient Egypt*. New York: Facts on File, 2003. Print. 17.

7. "Building a Pharaoh's Ship: Explore a Pharaoh's Boat." *PBS*. Public Broadcasting Service, Oct. 2009. Web. 8 Oct. 2014.

Chapter 8. Establishing an Empire

1. Bob Brier and Hoyt Hobbs. *Ancient Egypt: Everyday Life in the Land of the Nile*. New York: Sterling, 2009. Print. 255–256.

2. Rosalie David. *Handbook to Life in Ancient Egypt*. New York: Facts on File, 2003. Print. 271.

3. Toby Wilkinson. *The Rise and Fall of Ancient Egypt*. New York: Random, 2010. Print. 284.

4. Ibid. 285.

5. Rosalie David. *Handbook to Life in Ancient Egypt*. New York: Facts on File, 2003. Print. 292.

Chapter 9. The Legacy of Ancient Egypt

1. Zahi Hawass. "King Tut's Family Secrets." *National Geographic*. National Geographic Society, Sept. 2010. Web. 17 Sept. 2014.

2. "Pharos of Alexandria." *Encyclopædia Britannica*. Encyclopædia Britannica, 2014. Web. 17 Sept. 2014.

3. Margaret R. Bunson. *Encyclopedia of Ancient Egypt*. New York: Facts on File, 2002. Print. 214.

4. "History & Culture." *NPS.gov*. National Park Service, US Department of the Interior, 14 Sept. 2014. Web. 17 Sept. 2014.

5. Ibid.

6. Rosalie David. *Handbook to Life in Ancient Egypt*. New York: Facts on File, 2003. Print. 9.

INDEX

ABOUT THE AUTHOR

Lisa Amstutz specializes in writing nonfiction for children. She is the author of more than 20 books and many magazine articles. Lisa enjoys learning fun facts about science and history to share with kids. Her background includes a bachelor's degree in biology and a master's degree in environmental science.

ABOUT THE CONSULTANT

Elizabeth McGovern is an art historian and archaeologist specializing in the culture of New Kingdom Egypt. She enjoys teaching and writing and has excavated in Egypt at the site of Abydos, the burial ground of Egypt's first kings. She has a bachelor's degree in anthropology and a master's degree in the art history and archaeology of ancient Egypt.